GW01086898

OPENING LINE:
AN AFFORDABLE POE1

Broken Sleep Books is a working-class indie publisher putting access to the arts at the forefront of what we do. Established in 2018, by Aaron Kent.

Selected Anthologies from Broken Sleep Books

CONTENTS

ISBN: 978-1-917617-97-0

Cover designed by Aaron Kent

Edited and Typeset by Aaron Kent

Broken Sleep Books Ltd
PO BOX 102
Llandysul
SA44 9BG

Opening Line

An Affordable Poetry anthology

Broken Sleep Books

SWEET, SWEET

finally! you've come to visit
sniffing out anger –

proffering pics of floofy dogs
because you loathe cats

oh! you teach aqua aerobics?
yeah – to not get wet –

it was at the heated poolside
that first time we met

do you remember? asking
not where I'm from from

instead to tell you bluely
would I be more comfortable

with ladies only
which you thought I was

it's so nice of you to visit!
seeking out anger

maybe I should perform some
since the news brings news

new to you as powdered sugar
on chain café pâtisserie

wholesome and early-
opening – just you can't boycott

I'm late
for the train.

REFUSING THE 'HEAVY BEAR'
After Delmore Schwartz

he's a big bear, but he's out of shape. with me
it's a full-time job. but still, he will not behave.
pint of honey, in a straight glass. and god, that
strip of thwarted gristle in the mirror is myself.
so bear, reverberatory furnace of my rage, we
meet again. muffled thrust of disappointment.
yet again. and you are back. with my best luck
mauled in your bald snout, with your bad-head
wagging its forecast of clouds. yup. he's a big
bear. his lot is a quandary of hot coals; wasp in
the ear that slowly maddens. he growls as he
grows. and he grows; swells out his sidling
bulk with any remnant sweetness shaved
from bone. he does not dream. he quarters
the carcass of sleep in the close cell of his
small, bear brain. the night, and its thick
cache of smutty panics, forcing him back
to the scrub. again. yet again. he drags his
devastated stoop away from desire. oh, rue,
bear! you are big, but you are afraid. fear's
accustomed cudgel is your home. you live
inside the sore head of your legend. you
are shuffled to the rear of every stingy
zoo. the bear is here, gathering like debt.
trembles beneath the wicked tit
of the moon. or lashed, goes loadedly
swaggering, swinging his tongue
like a peasant's flail. he is the very
heavy threshold of my failures. his
funeral moonstomp, clad in rusty black.
he is beside us now, as i talk of ending;
picking the crust from my voice with

a finicky claw. my days are awash
with his motley; his loud and loutish
maundering. he is so big. he will not sit
down. he will spit it out. each dishevelled
syllable. he will have my say, and eat it
too. so bear, we meet again. and every
morning. dirty bruiser's auger, slumped
on the bed. and your petulant belly rumbles,
bear. the noise enough to break my head.

NARROW ENTRANCE

Like a marriage, the country house
had been rebuilt repeatedly over
the ruins of previous structures. Among
the Waverley novels in the bedroom nook
were *Quentin Durward* and *The Fortunes of Nigel*,
our worthy alibi behind a curtain
for an impossible fumble while the children
bounced on a four-poster bed.
Idea for a Walter Scott novel,
I told myself drifting to sleep –
Farquharson, or, The Ensign's Return,
in which an old house restocks itself
one pistol, portrait and tartan rug
at a time, seething away all those years
in their auction houses before finding
their way back home, and I your narrator
the unexpected master of all. At
the local beauty spot, rare butterflies
went straight to the sightings stage
on the visitors' centre whiteboard,
allowing me to think, no, believe
I'd seen them myself. Rolled-up
parcel of preposterousness that she was,
Queen Victoria penetrated
the Burn o' Vat, that outsized
pothole emptying into Loch Kinord.
And here we were, the anniversary
couple ten years on, the currents
of life trickling away under our
feet but our reconnection
lasting for the moment at least
it took us to squeeze again
through that narrow, difficult entrance.

CIGAR BOX BANJO

Blind Willie Johnson could coax
music from a single string. God plucked a rib
and found a woman. Concert aria
in the gypsy song, long groan
of orgasm in the first kiss, plastic bag
of heroin ripening in the poppy fields.
Right now, in a deep pocket of a politician's brain,
a bad idea is traveling along an axon
to make sure the future resembles a cobra
rather than an ocarina.
Still there's hope in every cartoon bib
above which a tiny unfinished skull in
its beneficence dispenses a drooling grin.
The heart may be a trashy organ,
but when it plucks its shiny banjo
I see blue wings in the rain.

from My Black Angel: Blues Poems & Portraits,
Stephen F Austin University Press, 2014.

SUNFISH

Who wants to live for eons anyway,
watch everyone you love dissolve
while you keep shining, pissing out
the latest drops of the ocean
that's passed through your body?

I'd rather be a sunfish than the sun,
rather hop over stepping stones
in my cowboy hat than endure
like the serious mountains.

I can't answer the sky's questions
or the sea's. I light candles
because I love starting fires

that are small and temporary
like beetles, like flowers,
like most of us, common as days.

CLASH

This, in... I won't say the *heart* – in the *machinery* of things,
the hiss, tick and flex of it, the under-rumble
like the gravel shifting in a dog's throat
readying to spring...

In the flash at the back of my eyes, the saw-teeth of a migraine
like a gritted gearshift between spinning discs of light,
the spark shower they throw off, a squeal
in all the senses...

As a clearing in a maybe too bird-singing, too sun-humming wood
might shrink back from itself, as a silence might turn
on its heel, going sharp as a snarl,
more dangerous

for being just out of hearing – a June day, its gentleness curled
like a dog's lips from the teeth, a calm that's not
so much broken as in the instant
before shattering,

a wave's edge feathering, about to ex- and implode
into light, all things rushing as if downhill –
in fact, on, into life. The lithe beast
of life's contradictions

leaps out of cover at itself, we may flinch but we can't
turn away, where else is there to turn to?
caught in the grip of now between
the moment's pounce

and the pounce towards it of an apprehension, too wild
to explain, that this too might be peace,
if heart had mind, mind heart,
enough to see.

GRAPHOLOGY SUPERSCRIPTION 106:
APOTHEGMS OF BURN

To the idiots who deploy their 'get
the best footage' drones over bushfire

emergency zones, hindering efforts
to bring things under control, I say

that it's a case of arson after the fact,
and that the fire of your imaginations

burns us to bone, the swirl
of props fanning the flames.

IN JUNE

In June, outrageous stood the flagons on
the pavement which extended to the river
where we spoke of everything except
the fear that would, when habit ended, be
depended on. Our fear of darkness as
the fear of darkness never ending. To
hell with it, you said, and why not? Let's buy
a dirty and slobbery farm in Albion. What
country is this? There was the big loom
we little mice were born to tarry in.
Its patter made the bad things better. O
we sang against the light as we sang
against the battens! Cold that June and mist-
shapen, the river mind and all else matter,
I called you. Where are you? It's getting
dark. But these being statements, they ran
away before I could say *hummock coastline theft*.
This is where we used to speak of everything.
I need one more hour please. One more
hour. My affordable memories sold, I hung
my phone from the highest flagpole and kissed
the face of England once discreetly, though
it wasn't you and neither was the mist
wherefrom in dingle darkness buzzed a single
notification. Call me when you get this.
And see I'm calling now, whether or not
this is *now* or *in time*.

i.

So. This the logic past injury.
An alcove to plant labor else
where. Givingness without
the given. Let thy name be near.
There is no fear of fear here. Where
we return. There keeps showing up here.
Speaking of what even Saxons knew.
Red-gold, green-gold, the difference there.
If I speak of suffering it is to leave it behind.
Two coals. Your mouth opens into mine.
Cleaving. Vines turn sunward to you. Wind
passes me o'er. I thought I heard you there.
Despite the permissiveness of the times, words
remain forbidden. The wind passes me o'er.
Names remain.

A FORM WITHOUT ITS SHAPE
after Daniil Kharms

There was a swelling but nothing broke through.
Only this theoretical tooth, lacteal, an absence.
There was no tooth because no mouth,
no mouth because no head, no head
because no body to befriend it.

And no thumb and no sucking of it. And no ear
at all, though the fossil of an ear on my forearm.

As a walnut has a socket, so a bed the dint
of a sleeper, so slow glass billows to the ball.

As to 'who' that was – don't ask me.
Even the question is without meaning.

SMALLER THAN THE RADIUS OF THE PLANET

There is a patch like ice in the sky this
evening & the wind tacks about, we are
both stopped/fingered by it. I lay out my
unrest like white lines on the slope, so that
something out of broken sleep will land
there. Look up, a vale of sorrow opened by
eyes anywhere above us, the child spread out
in his memory of darkness. And so, then, the
magnetic influence of Venus sweeps its
shiver into the heart/brain or hypothalamus,
we are still here, I look steadily at nothing.
"The gradient of the decrease may be de-
termined by the spread in intrinsic lumin-
osities" —the ethereal language of love in
brilliant suspense between us and the
hesitant arc. Yet I need it too and keep
one hand in my pocket & one in yours,
waiting for the first snow of the year.

CUSHIONED

Last night I fell into the airspace
over Gaza
and, suspended there,
plucked rosehips
from circling clouds
of smoke,
            made offerings
through prayer-hands,
                        lowered eyes.
And though I raised your banner
with the others
the ash continued to climb
            in pangs
                        of crimson, olive-green,
until there you were, again,
standing at the foot of the bed.
You were hungry, you said,
couldn't find the light switch
in the dark.

THE BUTCHER OF EDEN

Now God made Adam and Eve coats of skins and dressed them.
  — *Genesis 3:21*

And when he was finished,
he scraped fat
from the backs of stretched skins,
wiped the blood,
sewed the seams,
bit the thread with teeth
and said:
Dress yourselves in these.

And they said:
what is this verb?

God shoved his knife into the earth, and said:
It's like make believe
but for your body.

They looked at all the meat
still steaming
from when it was alive.

God said: Eat.
And watched while
beasts of Eden fed
on beasts of Eden.

THE OVERMIND

I was wearing a jellyfish over my head. I could barely see at all—
must have fallen down a basement aleph, bumping off the steps.

I imagine it was the same way I fell when my mother was pushed,
my foetus six months gestational inside her. The sting made my skin

feel like it was being flayed and when I opened my eyes, I saw
the walls shudder, as if mid-quake. I asked the doctor, what is

the distance between curse and symptom and she wrote out
her reply on a prescription pad: *it's like trying to measure the smell*

of death. June, the air thick as tar, a sixty foot truck came rolling off
Shore Drive onto 67th, smashing the side of the cab. I saw it all

in slow motion, wearing my jellyfish cape again, a tunnel of pixelated
shrapnel, the taxi driver's airbag an exploding green mushroom.

Someone groans. Who are you? Face pressed against the glass, blood
on the dash. *Turn off the ignition, turn it off,* then doing it myself, but

unable to pull him out. I emerged from the sky-tilted passenger side,
as if opening the escape hatch on a submarine, and jumped down.

A fireman mummified my hands, and we stared at the battered cab,
the driver cut from the windscreen before shock-vomiting onto the verge.

Glowing red and white in the ambulance light, a young medic said:
you were lucky, most people don't crawl out of those. I wanted to call

my daughter, Gaia, realising I could still hold her in my arms, see her
grow. Thank you. It is October, I have returned the jellyfish to the sea.

You've been given another chance said the doctor (strange term for anyone
on the brink of divorce). To survive, I must decomplexify everything:

no cigarettes, no meat, no wine, no love (not yet). It's too early to say
how things are going. One day I might wake up and not feel the sting.

MOULT

You say we're the sum of our
Ancestor's parts, of our heritage
as reckless abandon. I swear
I can be more than the late owl
as omen in refined sunlight,
or a bell struck for early winter.

In the eclipsing of our sleep
patterns we learn to abide by
the hole in the ceiling, through
which Jupiter swells and fills
what little room we have left
for night's impossible ballet.

Spirits wander as I wait
with you for all that may,
and all that will, endeavour
to hurt the things we love,
and so I hold you for the song
of both starlings and starlight.

OXBOW LAKE

I praise my mother's waters patrolled by piranhas,
their flanks glittering with gold flakes –

she was only warning me of the dangers of the world.
I praise the vampire fish, all four feet of him,

his sabre fangs, for he eats piranhas, just as one
big worry will eclipse smaller ones.

I praise the horned screamers perched
above her oxbow lake, their ghostly screams

preceding a storm, and the hoatzins crouched on overhangs,
their hoarse calls like nervous coughs –

their parents were only concerned their claw-
winged chicks might fall into the pool below,

where a caiman lurked, his snout nudging waterlilies.
I praise the giant river otters that made their dens

in her banks, how they worked like a family of troubles
when the jaguar paddled too close, biting him

until the water foamed red. I praise her jaguar-devouring
waters where my hand and foot buds grew

but wanted to shrink back into my trunk, my eyes that tried
to squeeze back into my brain.

For my days and nights are haunted by those otters.
For the vampire fish still surges from the depths.

For her carnivorous flesh flashed with fireflies
as the piranhas thrashed faster and faster, until the surface

churned with that feeding frenzy I call my birth.

WHEN SPELUNKING FORGOTTEN DREAMS

Stop just before the entrance, the sheet of running water or loamy smell. This is the last sunlit station; the rest is groove. The architecture of the cave helps people and animals sync up with space-time as well as with each other, like the internet shapes our built and social environments and is shaped by them. The finest paintings are far from the entrance, but no one controls the buzzer, you can call your way in. Call then; utter any silent sound or informational noise, the cave will respond. A little away, a little away; come close, come close. You can trust this voice, can you? You can hear your way to belief, the deeper you move in its stuff. Brush fingers, sticks, and bones against stalactites, compare the effects to xylophones or soundbars or whatever feels right to your sonic context. Stamp your muddy handprints on the walls, ceding your subjectivity to speleothem. Feel your way into millions of years of drip, flow, gush – never dry, never still – even if you cannot perceive the wetness and movement with your fingers, ears, nose – you can, you can. A shimmering carpet of crystals; an assemblage of golden eagles, porcelain skulls, bio-glitter, bhindi glue, lip melt, flute, fur. Every sound in space-time still resounds; every sound ever made leaves a scratch in the field; the field is the recording, every sound ever made reproducible. The air swathes warmer here, breath ripples further than you intended to go or thought possible. Maybe you'll ignite a torch to signal reciprocity; maybe you'll awake surrounded by bear scratches, horses, birdcages, shapeshifters, or by bears, artists, ceremonies, spirits. Will you dance, will you boggle, will you enter another kind of sleep? Here you are folded in; you cannot see or be seen, you are out of the state's earshot, beyond cannons and espionage. Here you can sleep for millions of years; borne by your secrets which will never be mined. You are the matter in which splendour is hidden; you are the sculptor who shrouds their work.

FROM 'GAZA, TIME'S BODY': I

Grab the poem by force
Grab it from the hand that writes

From the alif to the yā'
Those are letters with no hearts

The first a dove with no nest
The last the vocative for a nest

Devastation unhinged
Thirsty throats and rasped noises

Death with a muted heart
Is the Arabic for another home

TATE AND WOODS

The first thing Tate notices about Woods is the velcro shoes;
Size 11 velcro shoes, like a giant boy perennially held back.
He tries not to judge. 'You always been a detective?' Woods asks.
Tate stirs a second sugar, scoured from the pot, into his black coffee.
'No,' he says. 'In another life I wrote eleven detective novels.'
'Anything I might have heard of?' 'Anything you might have heard of?'
Tate says. 'No. I don't imagine you've heard of very much at all,
let alone one of my eleven detective novels.' 'I'm quite partial
to detective novels,' says Woods, a little hurt. 'Did you write
under your real name?' 'My nom de plume was Tyler M. Blanchard.'
A motorised street sweeper roars as it passes their table so that Tate
has to repeat Tyler M. Blanchard, screwing up his face as he does.
'Blanchard,' says Woods and leans back in his chair as if to dip
deeper into his memory. 'No, can't say I ever picked one up.'
'Well, no,' says Tate. 'I wrote eleven paperbacks published by
Gun Dog Press and then they folded and my sales
weren't impressive enough for anyone else to take me on.
Natural for a writer to become bitter in such circumstances,
but I can objectively say that my work was too sensitive,
too conceptual and too intellectually engaged for the average reader,
or at least for Gun Dog's average reader, to whose vulgar
appetites I refused to cater. I didn't even get paid
for my eleventh novel because Gun Dog had gone
into administration.' 'What was it called?' 'My last novel?'
'Yeah, what was it called?' 'Made for Sorrow.' 'Made for sorrow.'
'It sits molding,' says Tate, 'in a dozen crates in a bolted warehouse.
It is always snowing, in my mind, when I picture the warehouse.'

GLIMPSED GLORY: PORTOBELLO RUGBY
FOOTBALL CLUB

Let this be the first brick to the bridge across the water
crawed Kieran, *el capitan*, on the cusp of a win

after a pulverising run of losses – his jaw jutted
ugly & mean as a threatened eel, but our eely

warlord, our studded juggernaut. If there exists
a perfect poetry for each earthly moment –

the paragoning *ten-minutes-to-go-don't-fuck-this-up*
sermon – we had found our gunpowder plot.

Over the corpulent hoards we flung ourselves:
lunatic freaks of baby bristle.

Daniel, hurt hungry, da newly dead, tackling
as if wearing a stab-proof carpet. Shug,

released by the social, just for the day,
scrumming like a dodgem into a midden

of micro-machines. Wee scaffy Fred,
home haircuts & free school meals, sprinting

steady as a teenage Terminator. How quickly
the sands shift when thrust a little faith

from the sidelines. Us teenage strays, steeled:
against cudgel-limbed ogres

& the stopwatch's harrying; against the memory
of the staunch Canadian army cadette

who mowed us down blithely as carboard
cut-outs, staking try upon try, doubling

our vision then reappearing glistening
like the ice-lolly effigy of a god, a psalm

carolling off his lips: *don't stand on the tracks*
when the traaaaaaaaaaain's coming through. No,

not even The Train, that bulging headcase,
could stymie the day's fierce want. For Kieran

– who it turned out was not the eel but king
crow, beaking it back – had ruffled our feathers

chrome gold, & so we bricked that bridge
together, never worthier of the post-match feast

(flat pints, cold pies) we were on other days
too haunted or hopeless to claim.

NATURE POEM

I've seen the world and I have seen people. In flesh and on television.
I love all of nature. There are such colours in it, such people.
I can rest in green moss, sharp bites of wood in the forest scrub, listen
to the song birds' spits, calls of next door's kids yelling in the street.
They feel the sound of the word *mother* on their lips. I've heard her scream
at them. Wild and primate things. The cost of living is extreme. I see flowers
on the net, posted by friends with great gardens, such blousy ranunculi,
peony, Lily of the Incas. How they startle into life. I have seen the world.
My friend says *go out into the world – it will give you strong words, and such
romantic feelings*. Perhaps I will gush with wild, swelling floods, and become
alive *as if I am not alive now*. I have seen the world, in flesh and on television.
Once I swam naked in Lake Malaren as lighting struck the air, made runes
in the sky. I watch a young man on television, who'd been a boy-soldier,
kidnapped by men in the bush, he's blown the heads off men, ripped women
in half. I see his mimesis on the dusted street, his vital dance after
they rehabilitated him in Kinshasa, steps to piece his mind back. He dances
to keep living. Here is life invincible. Every day he makes a deadly jig
of kicks and gun-finger flicks. Passers-by mutter *there's the boy who shot
his mother*. I love that boy. I am a lover of nature.

ON IRRATIONAL HOPE

That when that day   a miracle will catch
Me and preserve my life when that day come
An unseen   flaw a rock explodes the hatch
And artificial weather rushes from
The capsule into space   and instruments
Experiments   and samples and the crew
Rush into space   as the space capsule vents
Its purpose   and I my   legs slipping through
The jagged hole I   grab a safety rail
Itself half-ripped   from the wall I haven't got
A helmet on   a suit   that death will fail
Universe fail   in just there   that one spot
And for a second lifetime failure keep
Me   clinging like a dandelion seed
Left lonely by wind   though the flower sleep
After the wind has taken off its head

APATHY CATALOGUE EXPLORATION

Dear garden full of stones and clay, I apologize for the neglect.
I have watched young stalks rupture the surface of your soil,
felt sunlight wrap around your body as attentive lover, as
palliative care for neatness. All heatwaves are sent to break
the wills of people too punch drunk to stand, or reclaim bricks
stolen by the landlord's newest plot. Windows peer outward
onto patchy lawns and lamplit driveways, our skins a striking
strip for the sparks of a match. Good appetites are present and
so is this grinning corpse. Remnants of the night sloshes in the
bowl, ice cream as fuel for late-stage capitalist enterprise. You
cannot hear without sound, but still, we love to see the gore.
We think about that old tree slouched out front, plant instead
Rosaceae, its blossoms apple pink like clockwork in the spring.

cute

one day, if luck allows, i will be old old,
and teenagers will call me cute for doing things
i have always liked to do, the way we call
toddlers and babies cute for doing things
like dancing, and they'll post patronising videos
of me and my cute friends cute dancing
with hashtags like grannygoals
whether i have grandchildren or not
and if i do, those grandchildren will use me
to make their tiktok videos funnier
or whatever media they use then
and the comments underneath from people
who do not know my favourite jokes
will call me sweet or adorable,
as if old age makes you comedy,
and if i continue to wear clothes that are colourful
i will be labelled brave or adventurous or outrageous,
and young photographers will stop me in the street
and call me fantastic, simply for putting on an orange jumper
and in the social club or care home
i'll be forced to do jigsaws and watch little children
from the local school singing badly
and the staff will bend down to talk to me
palms pressed on slightly bent knees,
and ask me if i enjoyed that, they'll say
wasn't that just lovely, hollie,
and i'll say, oh yes, what a treat it is

MURMURS TO BURIAL

Eat an apple with no hands in a window.
The train rumbles though Bavaria.
After, we have a brush with Kitty.
The scenery really takes a bite out of me.
She means the air.
I'm thinking of your head.
Not of you, but just the head part of you.
How it hovers like a ruined cloud.
The shuttering sky zoning out.
Bear down, death, ease on down,
surround us, ovally.

IGNEOUS INVISIBILITY

To live for the mystical leap, for divine alchemical combination
one must cross this worldly ring with buzzing imperturbable
utopian aristocracy, able to live within the basic understanding
that time has been exploded and the dragon of doubt been
de-nuded along with plutonium geysers spurting rattlesnake
combining as verbally engendered strychnine magic, that literally
turns igneous realizing from their astral geysers ascendant
perpendicular morphine plumes, thus one speaks of a cosmic
revolutionary who engenders by this act plasticity whereby
immortality leaps like a flying gunnar from the habitual proclivity
that is death, and the earth becomes one quick silver paradise
of haunting, and not and not unlike a scribe of paradise and
without flexion calculation as instantaneous existence, not unlike
incalculable hibiscus blizzards, the revolutionary within this
ethereal degree, of excess as power seems snared in luminous
monsoon rain, that transmutes to natural solar psychology that
progressively links the temporal with the a-temporal, as one
ringing global diphthong ladder, thus the voice of consciousness
becomes an emblem, becomes a discontinuous Eddie that
suddenly fuses as inward novocain phantoms, not unlike whispers
from totality alive in the hieroglyphic chambers of the blood,
not only contagion between being and non-being, but between
generations beyond human conception, symbolic of primeval
patterns and other space-time connective whirling as unknown
galactic symbology, that organically signals organically signals
the unimaginable that empowers incessant magical vapours
of the spiritual Sun, with its infinite bird space that looms and
transmutes, the damaged nerves of reflex, of human habitation as
it opts for vainglorious presentation, as it opts for false imperial
grandeur, with the soul blanked out by the body, the spirit
seemingly summed by religious erasure, and what prevails are
planetary provincial kingdoms summed by religious erasure, and
each part of their spectrum, hoards a kinetic ideal, provincial

kingdoms, and each part of their kingdom hoards a spectral
ideal, thus a private human state of privatized self-capture, and
the bloated state of privatized self-capture, drafting the soul with
interior spotting as static, therefore procuring an agreement to
keep the apocalypse brewing, exploring form between primordial
thrust and the form it engenders, so that death seemingly vanishes
as brinkmanship flailing, or simply a cross between both, never
as simple or believable logistic, there persists absorption of mind
in the metrics of peril, of clotted skeletal cinders, for scouring
the very habit and movement of destiny, yet there is a qualitative
kinetic, of genuine realia into seeming disappearance, not unlike
a horned wildebeest swallowed by a serpent, the former warped
by twisted microbes as lesions, resulting in opaque geriatric
compounds, being a maze as a form of psychic muscular arthritic,
of myopic leukemia, yet there persists existential challenge to
surcease, not only plaguing biological considerations within
metaphysical isolation, yet, operant beyond cellular hallucination,
as the empyrean invades the principle mind with Stellar spores,
transmuting to lightning-like power being intergalactic dawn
beyond de-limited human dialectic, at one with instinctive
threading, fused with the arrow of eternity, being aural yield
as supra conscious possibility, thus heliocentric immortality in
the cells, as looping architectural certitude, perhaps ghost as
ascendant hawk that ascends through the icy altimeter of the
Trojan planets, sans power as verbal centigrade, sans poisonous
nitrogen kilometers, these being specifics of optically strangled
ghosts, within the disappearance of silvered sun traces, not as
a dispersal of remnants, but into transparent consciousness,
as magical torrent seeping into primordial crevasses, etching
subdued flare by osmosis, not as in dense micro-biological
wooden blazings, not unlike having the power of a transmuted
Heron as it rises into amorphic infinity...

TEETH

The listicle, Fifteen Disgusting Facts About Your Body,
includes an x-ray of a baby's skull, complete

with milk teeth stacked up like jaunty tower blocks
inside the bone holes. Did You Know,

says number nine of the listicle, that women
are born with all the eggs they will ever own?

It's exhilarating to know what I'm capable of
shrugging off, how every minute is an act of giving.

The other women in the clinic look like they've given
up their bones and muscles too.

We lay in our recliners like dead dolls. None of us
knows how to transcend tenderness yet

and when it's time to go home, I look down
and see I haven't got my shoes on.

SAY TO MY PYRE THAT I WORE ONLY GOLD TO DEATH

not that I came to this island with blood smeared between
my inner thighs / not that in the wind-whip of the atlantic
the word 'indenture' sounded like brass coins, crumbling
to dust / not that my husband could have been any of those
men on our ship, watchful and wet-tongued, but Durga
in her wisdom found me one who was kind / not the colour
of my first sari bought in Trinidad, saffron bordered
by a rough umber hem / not the two teeth I lost in my thirties
to the blunt end of a scythe, hot breeze whistling through the gaps

not even that I stood in the canefields, sweat staining the bound thicket
of my breasts / the ache of my third baby against my bladder, seeing
the sunset bleed yellow across the Caroni / falling over fields of sugarcane
and the ghosts of good, murdered wives / not even that I still hear them in
my eighties, and the longing in their voices is molten, sunny as fresh dhal,
glinting / off the surface of the green stalks like teardrops of pearling amber –

daughter, when you stand before my pyre with your hands full of poui, each petal
glowing as a tropic star in your grasp / know I loved well / know I journeyed here
to find you, dancing free in my womb / let them know as I burn in the open air

I wore gold, in my nostril / bright gold on my tattooed wrists / gold, hard-
fought and fearless, notched in the softness of each lobe / gold, grinning in
place of the teeth that labour knocked out / all my gold, gleaming fearsome
from this life into the next / rising up to meet me as the fire melts me down.

TOMASSO DE CAVALIERI ON LEAVING MICHELANGELO

for years I'd thought this would be easy

but now we're really in the knotty grooves

of it   I knew there was this sadness

that encased us   but I'd kept believing

we could chip it back   find ourselves again

young and beautiful   caught forever

in the glory of our youth   but life is

more complex than art   and this morning

I woke up   looked out at the vaulted sky

its cloudy brush-wash blue   and I knew

that all things break with time   that it was time

Michel   angel   go   you held the heavy

stone of me too long   some things cannot be

completed   sometimes love defeats us

SI HEI LWLI—LULLABY

'Where has the sky gone?'
Asked a little boy from Cymru,
his first time out in the dark—
' Gone to sleep, see— shush -sh--
it's under a blanket, night-light dimmed,
rest on your pillow cariad-- we're almost home.

'What is dimmed, mam-gu?
Dim byd bach
Dim yw dim tan y bore iach
* *
'Where has the blue sky gone?'
Asked a little one in Gaza,
night after night – frightened;
'Shush, sleep now my love.
see the pillow I found nearby?
'But why is the sky so angry?'
No, no fire-- no more – it's dimming now ,

What is dim--?
Sleep now, heaven above is tired too,
Hey, I'll hum it and you a lullaby goodnight,

Ah! Dimming? Just a word
Dim is dim- in such a dim world.

Dim: Welsh for 'nothing'

WINTER ROSE

There being nothing to look at
on the white page but for this
pressing weight, and something
that flowers in the deficit,
where to begin feathering
the emptiness from which I can
survey my limits? These late hours
are a cold medley of petals
on a rose stubbornly open
beyond its season, unspeakable,
like the terrible work of God's mercy.
There being nothing to add
and nothing as read, life keeps
moving in me like a childlessness.
My future, my lifeline in another
form withheld. Instead I create
conditions in which to thrive,
albeit in a time like ours when
to sing is easier than speaking.
There's danger in the setting
down of the unsettled ultimately
failing to fill this need. I want
to lift you up and hold you.
Song takes precedence again,
left to age and seep through any
dilemma, the pink breath of song
defrosting the tongues of winter.

LAY OUT YOUR UNREST

Lightning Source France
1 Av. Johannes Gutenberg
78310 Maurepas, France
FRHW012035020425
43084FR00003B/9

9 781917 617970